# Mustard Seeds

# Mustard Seeds

by: Daryl Horton

Abolitic, Elgin, South Carolina

Published by Poetic Abolition, an imprint of Abolitic.

For information contact the author at: www.daryl-horton.com

Cover, Photos, Art and Design by Daryl Horton

Printed in the United States of America.

First Edition: July 2019

Library of Congress Control Number: 2019909768

PRINT: ISBN-10: 1-945047-06-2 | ISBN-13: 978-1-945047-06-0

MOBI: ISBN-10: 1-945047-08-9 | ISBN-13: 978-1-945047-08-4

EPUB: ISBN-10: 1-945047-07-0 | ISBN-13: 978-1-945047-07-7

*I dedicate this book to my sister, Nefertiti Horton. Rest in peace sis.*

And the Lord said, If ye had faith as a grain of mustard seed, ye might say unto this sycamine tree, Be thou plucked up by the root, and be thou planted in the sea; and it should obey you.

- Luke 17:6

# Table of Contents

# Introduction

*"We must learn to regard people less in the light of what they do or omit to do, and more in the light of what they suffer." - Dietrich Bonhoeffer, Letters and Papers from Prison*

In this book of poetry, we peep through a window at the lives of various people encountering different obstacles in their lives. Each event seems to test the faith and the resolve of someone in some way. Through each event, we learn a little about how people's faith in God is shaped, what they learn, and how they react. We gain an opportunity to step into their lives, see what they see, feel what they feel, and hopefully walk away with a greater appreciation for humanity.

The question posed in this book is, "How would the many trials we encounter in life shape our spiritual perspectives?" Although the individual poems of this book are loosely connected by the central theme, an attempt has been made to assemble the poetry into four groups allowing the reader to transition through four distinct phases of any belief system. The four groups include the point at which (a) we learn to believe, (b) we question what we believe, (c) what we believe is tested when things don't go how we expect, and finally (d) we seek information as to what will happen when we die.

This book is not an academic book. Instead, it is a creative look at real-life events, how those events may have shaped what we believe, and what all of this has to say about our humanity. As you read these poems, imagine yourself in the skin of the characters and consider how you would respond.

# Part 1:

# Learning to Believe

# Birthday Wishes

FADE IN:

EXT. DETROIT WAYNE COUNTY - NIGHT

The calm of the pitch-black dark is interrupted by the SCREAMS of sirens.

EXT. HENRY FORD HOSPITAL EMERGENCY ROOM - NIGHT

An ambulance screeches to a halt next to the entrance of the emergency room. A security guard pushes open the slow-moving sliding doors as two men pull a stretcher with a woman atop it from the back of the ambulance, the woman thrashing about in pain. The two men move quickly, transporting the woman through the sliding doors into the emergency room.

INT. HENRY FORD HOSPITAL ROOM 223 - NIGHT

NARRATOR (V.O.)

Your birth,
announced by growing pains
Your mother,
after nine months of incubating his seed
Belly bloated,
like ripe fruit ready to burst
Skin stretched so tight,

little hands and feet appeared tattooed.
You were a recipe whose ingredients included:
a dash of love
a sprinkle of hope
a drop of fear
one-half cup of prayer and
one skillful doctor.

He told your mother *complications are expected:*
loss of sight
inability to learn
lame limbs and
possibly more
discovered only
after birth.

Asked if she still wanted you.
Your father didn't.

# Blind Faith

EXT. KINGS CORNER, NAMPA, ID - DAY

We HEAR the faint sound of tambourines and people shouting in the distance.

EXT. NEW TEMPLE FREEDOM CHURCH - DAY

The BANGING of the tambourines and people shouting have grown louder. Like the give and take of a discussion between two people, the shouting follows statements made by THE PREACHER every few seconds.

INT. NEW TEMPLE FREEDOM CHURCH - DAY

NARRATOR (V.O.)

*Faith is the evidence of things not seen;*
the Preacher shouted
from a small wooden box
flanked by several chairs;
old pieces of furniture
clad with inscriptions,
decorative designs,
and a red seat cushion
that looked as new as the day it was made
all atop a raised platform
often referred to as
the pulpit;

an insignificant little spot

in an auditorium-like space

of a small old church;

a small white building

nestled in the crest of a hill;

a place frequented often

which today swelled with

family and friends;

people either standing, sitting, or waving fans,

beating the air around their faces

like wings beating against the wind,

pushing hot air around fleshly mantles;

masks resembling beached seals;

veils slick with sweat,

the waving simply a motion of futility

like ants that

rebuild the piles of sand I kick over every Sunday.


I imagine myself someplace cooler where

belief didn't require blind allegiance.

# Religious Proficiency

INT. NEW TEMPLE FREEDOM CHURCH - CONTINUOUS

Several church members stand and sway back and forth, stomping their feet with each statement the preacher makes while others sit, nodding heads and clapping hands in agreement with the preacher's every word.

NARRATOR (V.O.)

Church was a strange place
like a dark void or some
recycling center littered with
weak bodies, empty pockets, and tired hands.
Old bodies moved slowly but steadily
under the weight of
baggage carried for many years.

*Come, lay your sins at the altar*, the Preacher would say.

One by one
the young and the old
stood from the hard seats
and like trucks entering a dump site,
left their baggage at the altar.

Church was a place people visited
to learn what it meant to

"stand on faith."
An oft-repeated word puzzle
I had yet to solve and
one that only got more complicated
when Bible verses were read.

*Faith is the evidence of things not seen.*

So, I should trust what I can't see?
I mean trying to understand anything
only got more complicated
as the preaching continued…

*You don't know him, but he exists*
*You can't see him, but he is there*
*You may talk to him and think you're insane*
*But you remember hearing that he cares.*

*You may pray to receive an answer*
*You may cry because he loves*
*Unconditional promises are made*
*You silently thank the one above.*

*You stand in need of something, so you seek*
*Remembering he said if you do, you'll find*
*Whatever you need just ask*
*And your prayers will not be declined.*

I could never make heads or tails

out of what was preached.
I just liked the way
he made things rhyme.

# Spiritual Initiation

EXT. NEW TEMPLE FREEDOM CHURCH - NIGHT

The lush lawn of the church is littered with several more cars than were there for the morning service.

INT. NEW TEMPLE FREEDOM CHURCH - NIGHT

The church is packed. Every isle holds several families. There is a full choir. The drummer, guitar player, and the organ player are all there. Many of the CHILDREN are seated up front in the first two pews. We HEAR the beautiful music and the voices of the choir.

NARRATOR (V.O.)

My first experience with the Holy Spirit took place during revival one hot Saturday evening. I was in the first pew with my brother and sister and a few cousins. Our bodies gyrating with the music of the organ, with each beat of the drum, with the sound of a thousand feet beating against the wooden floor of the small church, sweat glistening on our foreheads. The organ player, a woman whose skin looked like aged leather, begins to play that familiar rhythm, her nimble fingers gliding across keys, tapping into the vocal chords of sisters and brothers and husbands and wives as the low hum of individual professions climb the rhythmic scale, giving way to loud shouts of capitulations, people surrendering to the unknown force that drives these beaten and war-torn black bodies to appear here every week without fail.

The pace of the music quickens as feet leave the floor, bodies levitate for seconds at a time, some increasing their range while others increase the frequency of each jump, and like a scene from some old war bombing footage, people begin to lose themselves in a frenzy of wild movements, jerking and contorting their sweaty bodies, while others begin speaking in unknown languages: similar yet distinct flavors of vowels, consonants, nouns, verbs - varying in spiritual dialect.

The music grows louder.

The Preacher comes down from the pool pit to place hands on the foreheads of the faithful and the forsaken. No one is sitting any longer.

*Any moment now*, I think to myself, awaiting the signal.
*Let's go!* My cousin shouts.

Small feet dart to the wall-side of the long row of pews as we all run around the church like bodies doused in napalm  We circle the aisles shouting at the top of our lungs. My sister suddenly stops ahead of us, her arms flailing like a fish out of water, the Preacher with his hand like a net on her forehead. My brother stops next, starts shouting, tears bouncing off his cheeks and careening, tumbling down into the small pocket on the front of his shirt, and I become aware that everyone seems to be caught in the snare of the Holy Spirit except me.

I couldn't feel anything,
except left out.

Seconds pass by slowly like the long hand of a grandfather clock

tic, toc, tic, toc,

as an ingenious idea began to take root in my mind: *I'll just fake it.* No sooner had the thought sprouted leaves, I let my body grow limp and fall to the floor. Minutes later, pretending to wake from an unconscious state, I slowly raise my eyelids, happy to see so many people standing around me surprised that I finally had an encounter with the Holy Spirit.

# The Blue Shield

EXT. I-87 - NIGHT

Small Nissan Sentra moves down the road at 55 mph in a 65-mph zone.

INT. NISSAN SENTRA - NIGHT

A YOUNG BLACK MAN pulls over cautiously, turns on the recording app on his phone and lays it on the dashboard, then places both hands on the steering wheel, and says a prayer as a police officer approaches, flashlight in one hand, drawn gun in the other.

                    YOUNG BLACK MAN (O.S.)

The last day of the work week approached
with the speed of a turtle
but it was finally here and
feet couldn't wait to exit the door of this building.

No sooner had the clock struck midnight
keys were unlocking the door to my car,
Had no intentions of giving room for the boss to
find unaccomplished work for these hands to do.

With windows down and
music blaring, I
turned onto the freeway

unaware of the black and white waiting,

hiding in the shadows

like a lion for the lonely deer wandered off alone.


Not even five miles down the road

eyes were blinded by the flashing blue and red lights

bouncing off the rearview mirror

filling my car with thoughts of Terence Crutcher

gunned down by Officer Betty Shelby.


Mind began to search for the proper protocol

knowing the wrong move may be my last

understanding any fear this cop may have

will provide the needed justification to blast,


so lips began to pray.

# Revolution and Religion

EXT. ATLANTA, GA - DAY

Many cars travel up and down the busy streets of Atlanta, GA.

EXT. EBENEZER BAPTIST CHURCH, ATLANTA, GA - DAY

Tourists, led by a TOUR GUIDE, stand outside Ebenezer Baptist Church taking pictures of this famous establishment. A young kid asks why the church is so important.

TOUR GUIDE (O.S.)

Revolution and spirituality are
two sides of a double-edged sword.
Church provided a place to find
hope, hidden within the walls of the sanctuary;
a place whose foundation included soil rich in desire,
and like farmers, pastors cultivated the spirit of revolution.

Vernon Johns, a modern-day Zealot, ruffled the feathers of
The American Roman Empire, with his fight for civil rights.

Martin Luther King Jr., Vernon Johns' successor,
continued in the office of the minister-activists promoting revolution
all the way, to the office, of the President, with his fight for economic equality.

Ralph David Abernathy Sr. continued the struggle for equality
leading campaigns, marches, and demonstrations, advocating
for the disenfranchised.

Frederick Lee Shuttlesworth fought against American imperialism
as a gladiator in the war against segregation and various forms of racism...

Many more minister-activists fought for
our souls and our humanity,
our faith and our sanity, while
today's minister-pacifists seem focused on
their role in the community
regulating religion to collect
tolls for spiritual immunity
rather than letting freedom rain
they seek personal gain.

Even so, many still believe and
many are still willing
to fight
for a Revolution.

# Part 2:

# Questioning Faith

# The Subversion of Faith

FADE IN:

EXT. RICHLAND COUNTY - NIGHT

The calm of the pitch-black dark is interrupted by the SCREAMS of sirens.

EXT. BAPTIST HOSPITAL EMERGENCY ROOM - NIGHT

An ambulance pulls up next to the entrance of the emergency room. A security guard pushes open the slow-moving sliding doors as two men pull a stretcher with a woman atop it from the back of the ambulance, the woman unconscious and breathing through an oxygen bag. The two men move quickly, transporting the woman through the sliding doors into the emergency room.

INT. BAPTIST HOSPITAL ROOM 223 - LATER

The woman's three kids sit in the room with her. The eldest, her SON, is in deep thought, recounting the actions of the night.

THE SON (O.S.)

There was a time I believed everything the preacher said:
*Ask, and it shall be given.*
*Seek, and you shall find.*
*Knock, and the door will be opened,*
he shouted, like a bugle

with large jackhammer feet

stumping up and down the pool pit,

spit flying like

small torpedoes launching from dark lips,

sweat dripping,

sliding down the sides of thick brows,

one hand clutching the microphone tightly,

the other hand flailing, swinging a white neckerchief

as if to signal his surrender to the lively audience

the kind that, for a moment, resembled the pale faces that

crowded around burning black bodies in the deep south,

shouting and yelling with intense expressions of hidden ignorance.

Is this what the crowds did at the feet of Jesus?

Is this the faith religion offers?


He had everybody on their feet.


With that much passion,

how could anything he says be taken for anything but truth?

And I begin to understand the ignorance of whites in hooded sheets

who confer allegiance without question.


Without question…


We had just gathered around my mother,

Chief Executive of our weekly family meeting,

when heart began to beat irregular rhythms against her chest,

Lips had barely parted before

she grew stiff and fell back onto the bed.

Her body convulsed repeatedly until she

just

stopped

moving.


Confused looks gave way to fear as

our hearts attempted to

escape the confines of our rib cage.

For a moment,

our pleas for her to get up fell on deaf ears.


A finger twitched,

Eyes struggled to open

Lips barely able to part whispered:

*Call 911.*


I road in front of the ambulance.

It was 20 minutes before the white ambulance driver realized he was going in the

wrong direction.

It felt like he had never been in a black neighborhood,

as if his role in the saving of lives excluded people of color.


Christ never felt further away from me than he did on this night.

My ears grew deaf to the words of the preacher

and I began to question

anything

anyone

presented

as Truth.

# Dismantling Hope

EXT. U.S. ACADEMY, MEMPHIS, TN - DAY

The narrow streets feed a stream of cars into and out of a gate guarded by a Marine.

EXT. CAMPUS WALKWAYS, U.S. ACADEMY - DAY

Cadets, civilians, and military personnel walk the short streets between campus buildings. A bell RINGS, singling the end of one class and the start of another.

INT. MUSIC DEPARTMENT - DAY

A young AFRICAN AMERICAN CADET enters the music room and takes a position amongst the other cadets standing in three rows on elevated bleachers. The CHOIR DIRECTOR plops down behind a piano and demonstrates how she wants them to sing a song.

AFRICAN AMERICAN CADET (O.S.)

Fixing the flywheel on my 1976 hatchback Mustang was difficult.
Leaving home was a lot like that, but
like a drill sergeant on a parade field
mom drilled into us the value of an education,
so, college was important.

Selected as a candidate for the U.S. Academy,

my first day was surreal.
It was a day filled with
loud shouting…screaming…running,
shuffle here, shuffle there
carry multiple bags of many items up flights of stairs
to a room built for two.
A sea of more bodies than I had ever seen before.
My new world was expansive, but I felt so small.

Daily praying blistered my knees but
tongue, ceaseless in its effort, begged
God to help me find a community;
a place where I didn't feel so, alone.
A poster appeared on the wall
announcing choir rehearsal,
and it seemed like God heard my plea.

Walking into choir rehearsal felt like
the repatriation of refugees.
Black, brown, and beige faces greeted me.
The familiar smell of pomade and hair spray
almost brought tears to my eyes.
A smile like sunrise stretched across my face
as legs positioned body amongst the others in the choir.

The choir director's fingers
danced across the piano keys
creating an arrangement of notes
warming vocal cords in preparation

for the serious work ahead.

Like a set of playful birds,
vocal and chord progressions took flight
sambaed to Angola and Congo drums
beating beautiful bass rhythms
into the soundscapes of Amazing Grace.

The beautiful arrangement of notes;
the artful dialog between voice and instrument
was like the sound of angels singing;
was like light rain dancing on the earth floor;
was like the soft hum of a window fan on low speed,
all ended abruptly as the choir director halted everyone.

*Someone is off-key;* she said as she stood to her feet.
*Sing again.*
She crept slowly past each member of the choir,
Holding her ear close to the group listening
like a sonar for a specific wavelength.
Her feet came to rest in front of me,
My heart sank.
*Everyone stop!*
Jabbing a pointy finger in my direction, she growled
*I want you to sing by yourself.*

I took a deep breath,
an uncomfortable feeling
like a heavy winter coat

draped itself about my shoulders.
Mind tried to temporarily transport me
to a peaceful place;
a place where, when alone, I was the star
and my voice created the perfect pitch;
a place like, my shower.

With the image of the shower
firmly embedded in mind
lips parted and tongue took position
as lungs filled with air.
Chest compressed, forcing air through my voice box.
*A-A-Amaz-Amazing Grace,*
*how sweet the sound*, I bellowed.
*Stop!*
Forehead glistened with sweat as heart
beat new and erratic rhythms into my chest.
She jabbed a finger in my direction again.
*Step out to the side.*
*Honey, your signing is waaaay off key.*
*You'll spend the next few sessions listening*
*before I put you back in with everyone else.*

My coat of shame
heavier than ever before now
made the simple task of breathing
a very difficult chore to accomplish.
All those years I sang in front of the church,
Why didn't anyone tell me I couldn't sing?

I stood, embarrassingly off to the side
as the earth shifted
creating a deep gulf that widened
with every passing minute
until choir practice was over;
until I
could no longer
feel
the familiar warmth
of faith.

I never returned for choir practice.

# Assailing Christian Philosophy

INT. U.S. ACADEMY - NIGHT

Not one sound is heard in the halls cf the U.S. Academy. A handful of cadets move aimlessly through the hallways, strolling from one room to another.

INT. U.S. ACADEMY DORM ROOM - NIGHT

A young CADET sits in deep thought, staring at a page in the Bible.

CADET (O.S.)

Words are beautiful. Language is beautiful.
Reading is like sitting down at the local buffet
to order a plate of sliced clauses and diced phrases, only
instead of eating like an American, you eat like the French,
taking the time to savor every syllable and all parts of speech.

Church people read like Americans eat: very fast,
leaving little room to enjoy the dish placed before them.
They skim over the contents, take what they like and
discard the rest as if the Council of Nicea made a mistake.

Like the educational system
Sunday school was an institution of indoctrination
complete with competitions often held
and prizes always awarded

for simply memorizing books in the Bible or
repeating certain scriptures word for word.
I always won, but
Did I ever learn anything of any real value?

In school, we train eyes to read every word they come across.
When eyes fail to recognize the words they see,
fingers are instructed to
turn the pages of a dictionary or
flip through the sheets of a thesaurus
to identify the meaning of the word.

Whatever discoveries await, are processed
devoured by the frontal lobe whose job it is to
determine the purpose of the statement,
assisting in the process of learning.
Even Reading Rainbow did more with books
then Church people do with the Bible.

One of my college classmates showed me how.
Specific tools are required:
1 Bible Concordance
1 Bible dictionary
1 Bible encyclopedia
books of history from the time frame under study
paper, pen, and an internet connection.
This wasn't an Easter egg hunt,
it was a real journey of discovery.

My understanding of faith
was being
redefined.

# The Blue Shield II

EXT. I-87 - NIGHT - CONTINUED

Small Nissan Sentra sits parked off the road with a police car behind it.

INT. NISSAN SENTRA - NIGHT

A YOUNG BLACK MAN turns on the phone recording app and lays it on the dashboard, then places both hands on the steering wheel, and says a prayer as a POLICE OFFICER approaches, flashlight in one hand, drawn gun in the other.

YOUNG BLACK MAN (O.S.)

Cop stops short of my open window
*Don't move*, his voice crackled, *license and registration!*
Neck hairs stand as ears capture the sound of heavy breathing
The kind of breathing that singles excitement
like an adrenaline rush just before doing something foolish.

*Officer*, I reply hesitantly, *my license is in my back pocke*t,
*Registration is in the glove box*
*Reaching for either may give you the wrong impression.*

Body, a nervous wreck, shivers with fear
Sweat beads up on my forehead
As if I were in the garden of Gethsemane.

Side view mirror catches the slight grin and bulging eyes as

Stiff legs inch his torso and arms closer to me

Shaky hands nudge the gun against my temple

*You black bastards are starting to learn*

An unsettled southern drawl thick with hatred whispers

*Get your ass out of the car, boy*

*It's time I got a notch on my belt.*


I silently repeat the name of Jesus as

Door swings open,

my forehead rocked from the impact of his pistol

whip-like arms yank me to the ground

hands attempting to block sand from

entering eyes already blurred by pain

are quickly hammered by a baton

ears overhear a radio call

*Send backup immediately; he's trying to reach for my gun.*

My neck trapped under the weight of his boot

The smell of hard rubber soles floods my nostrils

Must have repeated the name of Jesus until

mind blacked out from lack of oxygen.

Woke up in a jail cell

Charges unknown.


Once you experience terror

at the hands of

Those who serve and protect

The world

never quite feels the same and

Faith, beginning to waver now,
leaves you
asking God
why.

# Medical Terror

EXT. SMALL HOME, LARAMIE COUNTY, WY - DAY

Light exhaust smoke oozes from cars in driveways as owners prepare to start the workday.

INT. SMALL HOME, LARAMIE COUNTY, WY - DAY

An OLD MAN lays unconscious in his home as his daughter rushes to call an ambulance.

                    OLD MAN (O.S.)

Eyes opened as alarm blared into the morning,
Shifted weight until knees rested on the floor so
lips could thank God for seeing another day.
Prayers continued until conscious was satisfied
body was properly clad in the whole armor.

Rose to my feet and
a feeling of weakness washed over me like
torrential rains.
An erratic pounding against my chest
sent shock waves throughout my body as
feet slipped, failing to balance the weight of my frame.

*Scalpel, please.*
*Forceps,*
*Scissors,*
*Ready the surgical hook.*

Awoke to doctors hovering over me,
empty organ bags sat open like post office boxes
ready to receive parcels from a non-donor.

# Justice Wears Shades

EXT. SUPREME COURT, WASHINGTON, DC - DAY

Crowds of people gather on the streets flanking all sides of the Supreme Court.
The American Law is on trial.

INT. SUPREME COURT, WASHINGTON, DC - DAY

The PEOPLE take their turns questioning the American Law.

THE PEOPLE (O.S.)

Only in America
does the law judge in a way that,
allows similar crimes
to be judged differently
depending on, the hue of one's skin.

Judges justify the justice delivered
through their flawed judgment almost jokingly
in much the same way the media portrays
criminals differently when born in different cultures
but who echo one another's crimes.

When the hue is white:
"Boys will be boys" but
When the hue is black:

"We should string 'em up and horsewhip 'em."

A 12-year-old white boy is just a child but
A 12-year-old black boy is a man.

A white woman with chest pains is having a heart attack but
A black woman with chest pains is simply experiencing discomfort.

White school officials convicted of racketeering receive days in jail but
Black school officials convicted of racketeering receive years in jail.

Police politely approach a white man brandishing a gun
attempting to defuse the situation but
Police fire their weapons at a black man they believe has a weapon, killing him
only to find out
it was just his phone.

Only in America
does the law judge in a way that,
allows similar crimes
to be judged differently
depending on, the hue of one's skin.

Judges justify the justice delivered
through their flawed judgment almost jokingly
in much the same way the media portrays
criminals differently when born in different cultures
but who echo one another's crimes.

Justice isn't blind,
she's racist.

# Part 3:

# Unanswered Prayers

# Bruised Birth

FADE IN:

EXT. BAGGS CARBON COUNTY, WY - DAY

One poor, destitute chap pushes a grocery cart of junk down the street, while two other people at the corner trade money for drugs. The guy who takes the drugs darts down an alleyway littered with a handful of unconscious penniless souls.

EXT. CITY APARTMENT COMPLEX - DAY

Two people are engaged in a heated argument behind one closed door.

INT. APARTMENT 223 - DAY

A man draws back his hand while a woman, bleeding from the nose, holds her arms over her face to block his attack.

NARRATOR (V.O.)

Never knew my father but
always imagined him as
strong and
caring.
That description however
is best reserved for
mother.

Father spent his time
filling his veins with
the potions of the avenue medicine men;
the poisons of the street vendors;
the elixirs of death-dealing merchants;
the hawkers and peddlers of the short-lived escapes,
the kind father searched for at the bottom of bottles
rather than in the arms of my mother.

Even the best days seem to carry some gloom,
like sunshowers, a little bit of kindness
would break forth when
he would place cash in mother's hands,
a kiss on her cheek, but these moments
were as short-lived as his next high.

While some kids can recall
the voice of parents singing lullabies,
the caress of hands or the imprint of an ear
on the belly of their incubator,
My memories were of forceful imprints:
father's fists against the belly of my cocoon,
the angry voice of my junkie
demanding the return of the cash, he gave mother earlier.

Good days were often fleeting as
father regularly morphed, transforming from
Dr. Jekyll to Mr. Hyde,
anger discoloring his skin,

frustration wrinkling his brow.

My mother on the floor, screaming in pain

from fists, she could expect more attention from than lips.

Her only thought to protect the son she carried

from more pain, while blood streamed down her legs

unsure if it was her blood or mine.

# Molesting Faith

EXT. COMFORT LANE, DULUTH, MN - MORNING

A couple of rusty old cars move in opposite directions, their drivers waving to one another as they pass.

EXT. SMALL WOODEN HOUSE - MORNING

A couple of loud kids toss a football around in a nearby field, and a neighbor cuts his large forest of a yard using a riding lawnmower.

INT. SMALL WOODEN HOUSE - MORNING

A little girl, 9, suddenly turns, staring curiously down a dark hallway to see an older man, 47, summoning her.

NARRATOR (V.O.)

Begin the early years of life
trapped between the walls of love;
A small home made of wood,
Stacked bricks were steps,
The crawlspace a treasure trove of
empty cans and bottles of intoxication.
Comfort could be found here, hidden
amongst the many smiling faces, laughter, and tears.

Relatives.

So many relatives related through relations, relationships

seemed to prove the existence of a well-spring of affection.


No room too small to house a family.

No floor to dirty to provide a bed.


Children took out trash, washed dishes, raked yards,

cut grass, picked crops, and

if lucky enough

avoided him

except

my sister.

While the others got the lash

she got his love.


I think I know why everyone in the country is related.

# The Foolishness of Preaching

EXT. KINGS CORNER, NAMPA, ID - NIGHT

The quiet of the surrounding area is cut short by the SOUND of several crickets and other insects.

EXT. NEW TEMPLE FREEDOM CHURCH - NIGHT

A handful of cars claim spots on the lawn in front of the church. The lights from inside leave a yellow glow on the stained glass of the church windows.

INT. NEW TEMPLE FREEDOM CHURCH - NIGHT

A YOUNG BOY stands at the altar in front of the preacher, whose hand is on the boy's forehead. A few other people sit in the aisles, waiting patiently for something important to happen.

> YOUNG BOY (O.S.)

When the flesh is ready
the spirit will give birth or
rather when the flesh is compelled.

Forced to endure hours of praying,
the preacher refused to let me move
until I experienced what everyone else had:

A momentary loss of bodily control where
arms flail, body convulses, eyes roll back to search the mind
so tongue could utter a language never heard,
while someone more experienced
could translate, bearing witness to the words of God.

My knees ache. I rock back and forth, head bowed,
hands folded in front of nose,
tongue repeating the ritual incantation of the name of Jesus.
Nothing happens.
The preacher places his hand on my head
prays harder, pushing my head back and forth with such force
I swore today would be my last if something didn't happen soon.
Moments later
a twitch in one arm leads to the flailing of the other,
while feet repeatedly force legs into the air
tongue spoke an ancient dialect ears had never heard before.
Members sat in awe, some shouting, others stood stomping feet.

The preacher, pleased, eased the pressure
on my head and
in my heart
I felt bad for
faking it
again.

# Discarding Prayer

EXT. MILITARY BASE, IRAQ - NIGHT

A few ghostly figures, military personnel, meander in the dark. A flash of light escapes the flap of a tent each time it opens and closes.

INT. CONCRETE T-BARRIER, MILITARY BASE, IRAQ - LATER

A young SOLIDER is seated in the dark under cover of one of the T-barriers used as bunkers from enemy rockets. His eyes are shut tightly.

SOLIDER (O.S.)

In Iraq, I learned to reflect.
Discovered that prayer was just
another form of meditation
Designed to focus the energy
In a way that
Brings about change.

# Hopeless

EXT. ANOKA COUNTY, MN - DAY

Old cars drive by slowly as the old and the young stroll in and out of the local shops.

INT. SMALL DIRT ROAD, ANOKA COUNTY, MN - DAY

An old woman, 74, walks 3 miles from her house to the community church.

NARRATOR (V.O.)

Skin wrinkled, grew tough from
years of walking the same path
at the same time – midday –
for the same reason – hope.

She could only do what she knew how:
Feet carried her ailing body to the altar every day
so that tongue could beg God
for the return of a missing son.

His death, printed in papers
years after she started her prayer march but
the ability to read escaped her.

No one who knew had the heart to tell her
he died, doing what she taught him:
Fighting for the rights of his people.

# Imprisoned Revolution

While the people continue to question the American Law inside, the crowds
outside form groups, rallying behind various speakers publicly listing the crimes
of America.

NARRATOR (V.O.)

I think I understand.
I think I understand what it must have felt like
for the slave to have his God-given rights violated
by people who claim to be God-fearing,
but whose hearts are more wicked than Satan
because even Satan had to ask permission
before he touched the body of Job and even then
he was only allowed to do so much.

I think I understand.
I think I understand what it must have felt like
for the slave to witness the murder
of his brothers,
the rape of his sisters
the sale of his children
and to be powerless
to do anything about it because
the same God-fearing people enforcing the law,

created the law.

I think I understand.
I think I understand why freedom
has to go into hiding,
Why righteousness
is judged, prosecuted, and sentenced
before the trial even takes place,
Why activists
like Leonard Peltier, Veronza Bowers, Ed Poindexter,
and countless others
are serving decades in prison
over TRUMPed up charges,
victims of government programs
like COINTELPRO and
government institutions
like RACISM.

I think I understand.
I think I understand why
the real followers of God
lose faith,
stop praying
and take up arms.

# Part 4:

# After Death

# Temporary Flesh

FADE IN:

EXT. BALTIMORE HIWAY - NIGHT

A ceaseless river of cars travel the dark highways between Baltimore and
Columbia MD.

INT. SMALL NISSAN SENTRA - NIGHT

DOUG sits behind the wheel, driving slowly, blues music playing in the
background. He slowly lowers the radio volume. A blank stare covers his face.

DOUG (O.S.)

People often say
*You look exactly like your great grandfather.*
He was buried next to the church
The one down the dirt road that, just last year
was being swallowed by all the precipitation that fell.
Coffins emerged from deep within the ground
floating on rivers of rain.

Small ideas of what the world was like
gave way to greater understanding
once feet carried me far away from home.
Experienced long hours of deep studying

with brothers whose faith was as vast as an ocean.
Begin to learn things never once spoken of in church.

Met with the wisest man on earth.
Not physically
but mind could never get enough of devouring his printed words.
Apparently, death is but an illusion,
A temporary state of being since
there is nothing here that hasn't already existed
or will ever exist.

Maybe I am my great grandfather.

# Rendering Death Powerless

INT. SMALL NISSAN SENTRA - LATER

Doug maneuvers between slower drivers. Another blues song picks up just as the last radio commercial concludes.

DOUG (O.S.)

Death
We fear you
We fear you like deer fear lions
We fear you like children fear abandonment
We fear you like the rich fear poverty
We fear you like America fears the evolution of African Americans
We fear you like you fear life everlasting.

Death
We feared you, until
Christ delivered mercy
Delivered the opportunity to,
like Judges,
rehearse the righteous acts.
We feared you, dreading your appearance
with age
with acts of wickedness
with accidents
with and without cause.

We feared you, but
We fear you no more.


*Forasmuch then as the children are partakers of flesh and blood, he also himself likewise took part of the same; that through death he might destroy him that had the power of death, that is, the devil.*

*-Hebrews 2:14*

# Short of Finding Truth

EXT. AITKIN COUNTY, MN - NIGHT

The calm of the pitch-black dark is interrupted by the SCREAMS of Sirens.

EXT. TWO LEVEL HOME - NIGHT

A young man, MIKE, flips on the light in the bedroom.

INT. BEDROOM TWO LEVEL HOME - NIGHT

Mike paces back and forth in deep thought.

                    MIKE (O.S.)

Who was it that brought me to this place
All barren of life and love
Whose trees stand twisted against grey sky
The caress of another unheard of
Roots that dig in soil infertile
Lips like ice are cold
Winds that blow though trees move not
Words without sound made bold
Rivers run dry though clouds may rain
Like eyes that strain to cry
Death on earth is life in hell
Like sheep, we wait to die

The search for truth always in vain

Distracted by pleasure, she is never disdained.

# Everlasting Truth

INT. LIVING ROOM TWO LEVEL HOME - LATER

Mike moves to the living room. He continues to pace.

MIKE (O.S.)

I've often heard there is nothing new
But that which hath been before,
And our mind's eye no longer sees
Like a maze in which exists no door,
And we like babes born a new
Continue to learn and grow,
Though former things and former
Mistakes are those we don't really know.
Only records can show images of the past
And who we really are,
Though interpretations are many in number
The Truth is never too far,
 The search for Truth unlike the light,
 Never easy to find, though the switch is in sight.

*And if thy right eye offend thee, pluck it out, and cast it from thee: for it is profitable for thee that one of thy members should perish, and not that thy whole body should be cast into hell.*

*- Matthew 5:29*

# To Those Who Endure

EXT. FRONT PORCH TWO LEVEL HOME - LATER

Mike moves to the front porch. He stares up into the night sky.

MIKE (O.S.)

Within this land of dust rain never falls
Or at least it never falls when we expect
Furthermore, when it rains the ground bubbles up
And mud spurts like blood from a wound we protect
Like life in so many ways is this scene
Before these eyes, my life reflected in view
I struggle to survive the lows and the highs
Of the roller-coaster ride life takes us through
We try to separate the various lives we may live
Rather than allowing one to affect the other
As if we had conscious control over what can't be seen
For this prayer is the only thing providing shield and cover
      What we lack in strength we gain in faith
      Remaining strong to run this race.

# After Death...

EXT. FRONT PORCH TWO LEVEL HOME - CONTINOUS

Mike walks back into the house.

EXT. AITKIN COUNTY, MN - NIGHT

The calm of the pitch-black dark is interrupted by the SCREAMS of sirens.

NARRATOR (V.O.)

We bathe in the waters of peace

The wicked cease from troubling our souls

There the lash loses its power over my flesh

The police fail to force me to confess

No more lies, no more stress, no more fears

No more judgment by a jury not of my peers

There, even the weary find rest

The kind that arrests and even erases the hatred of racists

Governments lose the ability to capitalize on terror

Prisons lose the power to torture

No more incarcerations based on error or falsehood

The political enforcer won't create another Rosewood

The great and the small

The master and the slave

This is why so many desire the comfort of the grave.

Why died I not from the womb? why did I not give up the ghost when I came out of the belly? Why did the knees prevent me? or why the breasts that I should suck? For now should I have lain still and been quiet, I should have slept: then had I been at rest, With kings and counsellors of the earth, which built desolate places for themselves; Or with princes that had gold, who filled their houses with silver: Or as an hidden untimely birth I had not been; as infants which never saw light. There the wicked cease from troubling; and there the weary be at rest. There the prisoners rest together; they hear not the voice of the oppressor. The small and great are there; and the servant is free from his master. Wherefore is light given to him that is in misery, and life unto the bitter in soul; Which long for death, but it cometh not; and dig for it more than for hid treasures; Which rejoice exceedingly, and are glad, when they can find the grave?

*-Job 3:11-22*

# Acknowledgments

The works in this book include poetry written over the last few years of my life. It has taken me longer than I imagined to complete this project as I kept coming up with new excuses for why so much more needed to be done. However, current and past events that threaten the very nature of what it means to be humane forced me to go back and review this work from a different perspective. Hopefully, you find that perspective both challenging and rewarding. I want to thank my family, who added to this project by appearing in the artistic photographs included in this book of poetry. I would also like to thank God for blessing me with the talent and gift of being creative.

# About the Author

Daryl Horton was born in 1976 in Detroit, MI, but grew up in Hopkins and Columbia SC. After graduating from the U.S. Naval Academy in 2000 with a B.S. in English, Daryl joined the U.S. Marine Corps and spent the next 11 years serving his country.

His educational background includes an MFA in Creative Writing from National University, a Masters in Information Systems Management specializing in business information management from Walden University, and a certificate of advanced graduate studies in Management specializing in Knowledge Management from Walden University.

Daryl has written for and participated in several writing forums, contests, and ezines where he sometimes writes under the pen names Subconscious and The Abolitionist. Some of the themes Daryl's work revolves around include spirituality, love, history, activism, and philosophy.

Find out more about Daryl at www.daryl-horton.com

# Other Books by the Author

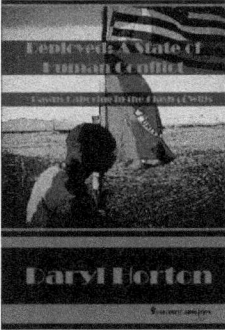

Deployed: A State of Human Conflict at Amazon (http://amzn.to/1qz66ZW).

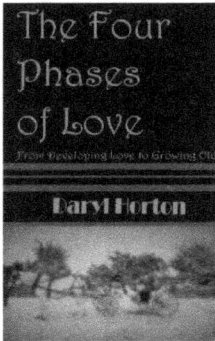

The Four Phases of Love at Amazon (http://amzn.to/1KvDAB0).